Barclay's Big Adventure

To Kelly Thankyou,

By
Kay Millard Hosmer

Kay Millard Hosmer

CreateSpace, a Division of Amazon.com
Seattle, Washington
2018

This book is dedicated to all
of my grand-children and great grand-children,
and especially in loving memory of all the family
pets who were not as lucky as Barclay, and lost
their lives during the fires.

First Edition
April 2018

Copyright (C) 2018 by Kay Millard Hosmer

This book tells the heart-warming story of how a little dog survived one of the largest wildfires in California's history.

Barclay lived on a quiet wooded lane and had a wonderful backyard.

Every day he would watch the squirrels tease the bluejays high up in the big oak trees.

Sometimes he could peek
through his fence and see wild
turkeys and their chicks

looking for food while walking
along the dry creek bed behind
his house.

In the late afternoon a doe,
with a pair of fawns who
were losing their little spots,
would often slip quietly past his
house, on their way to
getting a cool drink.

One day in October, Barclay's family packed to go on a trip. Their neighbor was going to take care of him and their cat.

That night, she settled Barclay in his dog house and he fell fast asleep, dreaming of tasty bones and treats.

During the night, the neighbor woke Barclay and grabbed his collar. She snapped on his leash. He knew it wasn't a good time to take a walk.

She hurried him out of the house and to her car. She tied him to the door handle and then went back into the house to get the cat.

The wind was blowing hot smoky air, which burned Barclay's nose and eyes. He pulled and pulled on his leash, which finally came away from the handle. Barclay ran and ran, with his leash trailing out behind him.

The neighbor came out with the cat, but Barclay was gone! She felt terrible and she searched and searched, and searched, but finally she had to leave.

Everyone else had already been evacuated. The fire was closing in on the area of his home from many directions.

The hills were glowing orange. Barclay's paws hurt, and his whole body ached. Barclay was now alone.

He'd run all night, and nothing around him was familiar.

Tears ran down his little face. "Where's my family, I'm thirsty and hungry" thought the little dog.

He saw a creek and walked down to it. Black flakes were floating on the water, and it tasted burnt.

His eyes were all blurry from the smoke. Barclay laid down, thinking "Where is my family? Where am I?" and he fell asleep.

A little later he woke up with a jolt. He sensed that something was very, very wrong. Just then, he saw a mountain lion jump on a big rock right above him!

Barclay knew that mountain lions meant danger. They stared at one another for a minute or two, and then the mountain lion turned and ran out of sight.

Barclay wondered, "Maybe she is just looking for her family, too" and so he went back to sleep.

Day after day passed. Barclay walked and sniffed all around, hoping to catch a familiar smell.

But, everywhere that he looked, all he saw were burned homes and vineyards.

"Where is my home? what has happened to my family?"

As Barclay came upon a road,
a big red fire engine came
speeding past him. They seemed
to be in an awful hurry.

"Here I am, take me to my
family." he thought to himself,
but they did not stop.

Barclay stood in the road, waiting for someone to help, but there was no one except a little skunk who waddled across his path.

It ran into the grass and turned to look back at him. "Oh, I don't like that smell! I think I'll go the other way!" thought Barclay. So, he turned and ran again!

That night Barclay fell asleep under a bridge. His dreams were filled with thoughts of his back yard and how he had escaped from the big mountain lion.

The next morning he woke up to footsteps. "Oh my family has come to get me!" he thought.

He ran quickly to the road, only to see a man who he didn't know.

The man seemed nice, so he followed him home. The man fed him, and Barclay fell asleep on their couch. It felt good to be in a home again, but he missed his cat and his own couch.

Things just weren't the same.
He was so very lonesome
for his own family.

One day, while the man was
walking Barclay, a man and lady
saw them and asked where the
dog had come from, as they
thought he looked familiar.

The lady talked to the man and, after some discussion, he handed Barclay over to the couple.

"Oh, they're taking me home," he thought.

But Barclay only went to the couple's home for that night.

"This isn't my family either." he cried. "I just want my own bed and my own family."

The following morning, the couple took Barclay to another lady who was really friendly. She even smelled familiar.

He could lay on her sofa and patiently watch out the window for signs of his missing family.

Barclay now had plenty of good healthy food and his water was nice and fresh.

The air was getting clearer each day, and his eyes weren't hurting as much.

It had only been a couple of weeks, but to him it seemed like he had been there forever. "Will I ever see my family again?" thought Barclay.

It seemed like an eternity, but one day, Barclay saw a car coming up the drive and it looked familiar! "Is that my car?" he thought.

"Yes, oh yes, that IS my car and that IS my family!"

He jumped for joy and ran to greet them. Everyone was happy to see Barclay, and he had such a story to tell them.

Barclay wasn't sure how he
was going to be able to do that.

After being helped by many kind people, the last lady had recognized Barclay, and knew that his family was away.

She called them with the news that he was safe. She kept him until the evacuation was lifted

and they could return to their home, which had been spared from the terrible fire.

Finally, Barclay was back in his very own yard! The deer came back and the turkeys roamed past the fence again. His cat was glad to see him, too!

Barclay is a very special dog
and was very, very lucky to
have survived his big adventure,
for, you see, he is totally deaf.

He could not hear people
calling him, or any of what
was going on around him.

Nor could he tell his family
what happened, so we have
tried to speak for him.

Author's Note:

Barclay is a real King Charles Spaniel that lives with his family in Glen Ellen, California. He really is totally deaf and he really did get loose during the fire by breaking away from the sitter's car door. She tried so very hard to find him but finally had to evacuate for her own safety.

This is our interpretation of his adventures, of his being rescued and returned safely to his home 14 days later, after the evacuation order had been lifted.

Photos of Barclay on the front cover, and on pages 11, 18, 20, and 24 by Caroline Hampton

Made in the USA
Lexington, KY
27 June 2018